Low-Carb
Desserts

Publications International, Ltd.

Favorite Brand Name Recipes at www.fbnr.com

Pictured on the front cover *(clockwise from top):* Cranberry Orange Cheesecake *(page 8),* Speedy Pineapple-Lime Sorbet *(page 56),* White Chocolate Pudding Parfait *(page 34)* and Currant Cheesecake Bars *(page 88).*

Pictured on the back cover *(top to bottom):* Frozen Berry Ice Cream *(page 54),* Easy Fruit Tarts *(page 22)* and Strawberry Bavarian Deluxe *(page 38).*

ISBN: 1-4127-2211-X

Manufactured in China.

8 7 6 5 4 3 2 1

Nutritional Analysis: The nutritional information that appears with each recipe was submitted in part by the participating companies and associations. Every effort has been made to check the accuracy of these numbers. However, because numerous variables account for a wide range of values for certain foods, nutritive analyses in this book should be considered approximate.

Microwave Cooking: Microwave ovens vary in wattage. Use the cooking times as guidelines and check for doneness before adding more time.

Preparation/Cooking Times: Preparation times are based on the approximate amount of time required to assemble the recipe before cooking, baking, chilling or serving. These times include preparation steps such as measuring, chopping and mixing. The fact that some preparations and cooking can be done simultaneously is taken into account. Preparation of optional ingredients and serving suggestions is not included.

Note: This book is for informational purposes and is not intended to provide medical advice. Neither Publications International, Ltd., nor the authors, editors or publisher take responsibility for any possible consequences from any treatment, procedure, exercise, dietary modification, action, or applications of medication or preparation by any person reading or following the information in this cookbook. The publication of this book does not constitute the practice of medicine, and this cookbook does not attempt to replace your physician or your pharmacist. **Before undertaking any course of treatment, the authors, editors and publisher advise the reader to check with a physician or other health care provider.**

Contents

Heavenly Cheesecakes

Strawberry-Topped Cheesecake Cups

  1 **cup sliced strawberries**
10 **packages sugar substitute, divided**
  1 **teaspoon vanilla, divided**
 ½ **teaspoon grated orange peel**
 ¼ **teaspoon grated fresh ginger**
  1 **package (8 ounces) cream cheese, softened**
 ½ **cup sour cream**
  2 **tablespoons granulated sugar**
16 **vanilla wafers, crushed**
    Fresh mint leaves (optional)

1. Combine strawberries, 1 package sugar substitute, ¼ teaspoon vanilla, orange peel and grated ginger in medium bowl; toss gently. Let stand 20 minutes to allow flavors to blend.

2. Meanwhile, combine cream cheese, sour cream, remaining 9 packets sugar substitute and granulated sugar in medium mixing bowl. Add remaining ¾ teaspoon vanilla; beat 30 seconds on low speed of electric mixer. Increase to medium speed; beat 30 seconds or until smooth.

3. Spoon cream cheese mixture into 8 individual ¼-cup ramekins. Top each with about 2 tablespoons vanilla wafer crumbs and about 2 tablespoons strawberry mixture. Garnish with mint, if desired.

Makes 8 servings

Nutrients Per Serving					
Calories	**205**	Cholesterol	**36mg**	Carbohydrate	**15g**
Sodium	**127mg**	Protein	**3g**	Fiber	**<1g**
Total fat	**15g**				

Strawberry-Topped Cheesecake Cups

Cranberry Orange Cheesecake

1⅓ cups gingersnap crumbs
3 tablespoons EQUAL® SPOONFUL*
3 tablespoons stick butter or margarine, melted
3 packages (8 ounces each) reduced-fat cream cheese, softened
1 cup EQUAL® SPOONFUL**
2 eggs
2 egg whites
2 tablespoons cornstarch
¼ teaspoon salt
1 cup reduced-fat sour cream
2 teaspoons vanilla
1 cup chopped fresh or frozen cranberries
1½ teaspoons grated orange peel

*May substitute 4½ packets Equal® sweetener.

**May substitute 24 packets Equal® sweetener.

• Mix gingersnap crumbs, 3 tablespoons Equal® Spoonful and melted butter in bottom of 9-inch springform pan. Reserve 2 tablespoons crumb mixture. Pat remaining mixture evenly onto bottom of pan. Bake in preheated 325°F oven 8 minutes. Cool on wire rack.

• Beat cream cheese and 1 cup Equal® Spoonful in large bowl until fluffy; beat in eggs, egg whites, cornstarch and salt. Beat in sour cream and vanilla until blended. Gently stir in cranberries and orange peel. Pour batter into crust in pan. Sprinkle with reserved crumb mixture.

• Bake in 325°F oven 45 to 50 minutes or until center is almost set. Remove cheesecake to wire rack. Gently run metal spatula around rim of pan to loosen cake. Let cheesecake cool completely; cover and refrigerate several hours or overnight before serving. To serve, remove sides of springform pan. *Makes 16 servings*

Nutrients Per Serving					
Calories	**196**	Cholesterol	**62mg**	Carbohydrate	**13g**
Sodium	**268mg**	Protein	**7g**	Fiber	**1g**
Total fat	**13g**				

Cranberry Orange Cheesecake

Chocolate Swirled Cheesecake

Yogurt Cheese (recipe follows)
2 tablespoons graham cracker crumbs
1 package (8 ounces) Neufchâtel cheese (⅓ less fat cream cheese), softened
1½ teaspoons vanilla extract
¾ cup sugar
1 tablespoon cornstarch
1 container (8 ounces) liquid egg substitute
¼ cup HERSHEY'S Cocoa
¼ teaspoon almond extract

1. Prepare Yogurt Cheese.

2. Heat oven to 325°F. Spray bottom of 8- or 9-inch springform pan with vegetable cooking spray. Sprinkle graham cracker crumbs on bottom of pan.

3. Beat Yogurt Cheese, Neufchâtel cheese and vanilla in large bowl on medium speed of mixer until smooth. Add sugar and cornstarch; beat just until well blended. Gradually add egg substitute, beating on low speed until blended.

4. Transfer 1½ cups batter to medium bowl; add cocoa. Beat until well blended. Stir almond extract into vanilla batter. Alternately spoon vanilla and chocolate batters into prepared pan. With knife or metal spatula, cut through batters for marble effect.

5. Bake 35 minutes for 8-inch pan, 40 minutes for 9-inch pan or until edge is set. With knife, loosen cheesecake from side of pan. Cool completely in pan on wire rack.

6. Cover; refrigerate at least 6 hours before serving. Just before serving, remove side of pan. Garnish as desired. Cover; refrigerate leftover cheesecake. *Makes 16 servings*

Yogurt Cheese: Use one 16-ounce container plain lowfat yogurt, no gelatin added. Line non-rusting colander or sieve with large piece of double thickness cheesecloth or large coffee filter; place colander over deep bowl. Spoon yogurt into prepared colander; cover with plastic wrap. Refrigerate until liquid no longer drains from yogurt, about 24 hours. Remove yogurt from cheesecloth and place in separate bowl; discard liquid.

continued on page 12

Chocolate Swirled Cheesecake

Chocolate Swirled Cheesecake, continued

Nutrients Per Serving					
Calories	**110**	Cholesterol	**15mg**	Carbohydrate	**12g**
Sodium	**100mg**	Protein	**4g**	Fiber	**<1g**
Total fat	**4g**				

Southern Peanut Butter Cheesecake

½ **cup low-fat graham cracker crumbs**
8 **ounces light cream cheese, cut into cubes**
8 **ounces fat-free cream cheese, cut into cubes**
½ **cup fat-free sour cream**
½ **cup fat-free ricotta or low-fat cottage cheese**
⅓ **cup peanut butter**
½ **cup firmly packed dark brown sugar**
2 **teaspoons vanilla extract**
6 **egg whites** *or* ¾ **cup egg substitute**

Coat 9-inch springform pan with cooking spray. Sprinkle graham cracker crumbs evenly over bottom of pan. Set aside. Process cream cheese, sour cream and ricotta cheese in food processor until smooth. Add peanut butter and mix well. Slowly add sugar and vanilla extract. Slowly pour egg whites through food chute with food processor running. Blend until combined. Spoon mixture over graham cracker crumbs. Bake in preheated 300°F oven for 50 minutes. (Center will be soft but will firm up when chilled.) Turn oven off and leave cheesecake in oven for 30 more minutes. Remove from oven; let cool to room temperature on wire rack. Cover and chill 8 hours. Serve with assorted fresh berries. *Makes 10 servings*

Favorite recipe from **Peanut Advisory Board**

Nutrients Per Serving					
Calories	**140**	Cholesterol	**10mg**	Carbohydrate	**14g**
Sodium	**240mg**	Protein	**13g**	Fiber	**0g**
Total fat	**5g**				

New York Cheesecake

1¼ cups vanilla wafer crumbs
4 tablespoons stick butter or margarine, melted
2 tablespoons EQUAL® SPOONFUL*
3 packages (8 ounces each) reduced-fat cream cheese, softened
¾ cup EQUAL® SPOONFUL**
2 eggs
2 egg whites
2 tablespoons cornstarch
1 cup reduced-fat sour cream
1 teaspoon vanilla
1 pint strawberries, sliced (optional)

Strawberry Sauce (optional)
1 package (16 ounces) frozen unsweetened strawberries, thawed
¼ cup EQUAL® SPOONFUL***
1 tablespoon lemon juice

*May substitute 3 packets Equal® sweetener.

**May substitute 18 packets Equal® sweetener.

***May substitute 6 packets Equal® sweetener.

• Mix vanilla wafer crumbs, butter and 2 tablespoons Equal® Spoonful in bottom of 9-inch springform pan. Reserve 1 tablespoon of crumb mixture. Pat remaining mixture evenly on bottom and ½ inch up side of pan. Bake in preheated 325°F oven about 8 minutes or until crust is lightly browned. Cool on wire rack.

• Beat cream cheese and ¾ cup Equal® Spoonful in large bowl until fluffy; beat in eggs, egg whites and cornstarch. Mix in sour cream and vanilla until well blended. Pour mixture into crust in pan.

• Bake in 325°F oven 45 to 50 minutes or just until set in center. Remove cheesecake from oven, sprinkle with reserved crumbs. Cool completely on wire rack. Refrigerate 8 hours or overnight.

• For Strawberry Sauce, process berries in food processor or blender until smooth. Stir in ¼ cup Equal® Spoonful and lemon juice. Refrigerate until serving time. Remove side of pan; place cheesecake on serving plate. Serve with strawberries and Strawberry Sauce.   *Makes 16 servings*

Nutrients Per Serving					
Calories	**158**	Cholesterol	**50mg**	Carbohydrate	**10g**
Sodium	**234mg**	Protein	**7g**	Fiber	**<1g**
Total fat	**10g**				

13

Chocolate Cheesecake

2 packages (8 ounces each) cream cheese, softened
2 eggs
⅓ cup plus 2 teaspoons granular sugar substitute,* divided
2 tablespoons honey
3 teaspoons vanilla, divided
2 level tablespoons unsweetened cocoa powder
1 cup heavy whipping cream

*Choose a sugar substitute that measures like sugar, such as Splenda® or Equal® Spoonful.

1. Preheat oven to 350°F. Spray 8-inch round cake pan with nonstick cooking spray. Cut 8-inch parchment paper or wax paper circle to fit bottom of pan. Place paper in pan; spray lightly with cooking spray.

2. Beat cream cheese, eggs, ⅓ cup sugar substitute, honey and 2 teaspoons vanilla in large bowl with electric mixer at medium speed 2 to 3 minutes just until well blended. With mixer running on low speed, beat in cocoa until well blended. *Do not overbeat.*

3. Pour batter into prepared pan. Bake 35 to 40 minutes until center is set. Cool 10 minutes on wire rack; run thin spatula around edge of cheesecake to loosen. Cool completely.

4. Invert cheesecake onto plate. Remove parchment paper. Place serving plate over cake; invert cake top side up. Cover loosely with plastic wrap. Refrigerate at least 4 hours or overnight.

5. Beat cream, remaining 2 teaspoons sugar substitute and 1 teaspoon vanilla in small deep bowl with electric mixer at high speed until stiff peaks form. Serve with cheesecake.   *Makes 10 servings*

Nutrients Per Serving					
Calories	**296**	Cholesterol	**125mg**	Carbohydrate	**7g**
Sodium	**158mg**	Protein	**6g**	Fiber	**1g**
Total fat	**27g**				

Chocolate Cheesecake

Rich Chocolate Cheesecake

 1 cup chocolate wafer crumbs
 3 tablespoons EQUAL® SPOONFUL*
 3 tablespoons stick butter or margarine, melted
 3 packages (8 ounces each) reduced-fat cream cheese, softened
1¼ cups EQUAL® SPOONFUL**
 2 eggs
 2 egg whites
 2 tablespoons cornstarch
 ¼ teaspoon salt
 1 cup reduced-fat sour cream
 2 teaspoons vanilla
 4 ounces (4 squares) semi-sweet chocolate, melted and slightly
    cooled

*May substitute 4½ packets Equal® sweetener.

**May substitute 30 packets Equal® sweetener.

• Mix chocolate crumbs, 3 tablespoons Equal® Spoonful and melted butter in bottom of 9-inch springform pan. Pat mixture evenly onto bottom of pan. Bake in preheated 325°F oven 8 minutes. Cool on wire rack.

• Beat cream cheese and 1¼ cups Equal® Spoonful in large bowl until fluffy; beat in eggs, egg whites, cornstarch and salt. Beat in sour cream and vanilla until well blended. Gently fold in melted chocolate. Pour batter into crust.

• Bake in 325°F oven 40 to 45 minutes or until center is almost set. Remove cheesecake to wire rack. Gently run metal spatula around rim of pan to loosen cake. Let cheesecake cool completely; cover and refrigerate several hours or overnight before serving. To serve, remove side of springform pan.   *Makes 16 servings*

Nutrients Per Serving					
Calories	**217**	Cholesterol	**62mg**	Carbohydrate	**13g**
Sodium	**246mg**	Protein	**7g**	Fiber	**1g**
Total fat	**16g**				

Rich Chocolate Cheesecake

Cool Lime Cheesecake

1 cup graham cracker crumbs
3 tablespoons stick butter or margarine, melted
2 tablespoons EQUAL® SPOONFUL*
2 packages (8 ounces each) reduced-fat cream cheese, softened
⅔ cup EQUAL® SPOONFUL**
1 egg
2 egg whites
½ teaspoon grated lime peel
3 tablespoons fresh lime juice

*May substitute 3 packets Equal® sweetener.

**May substitute 16 packets Equal® sweetener.

• Combine graham cracker crumbs, melted butter and 2 tablespoons Equal® Spoonful in bottom of 8-inch springform pan or 8-inch cake pan; pat evenly on bottom and ½ inch up side of pan. Bake in preheated 325°F oven 8 minutes.

• Beat cream cheese and ⅔ cup Equal® Spoonful in medium bowl until fluffy. Beat in egg, egg whites, lime peel and juice until well blended. Pour cream cheese mixture into prepared crust.

• Bake in 325°F oven 30 to 35 minutes or until center is almost set. Cool on wire rack. Refrigerate at least 3 hours before serving.

Makes 8 servings

Nutrients Per Serving					
Calories	**197**	Cholesterol	**58mg**	Carbohydrate	**14g**
Sodium	**366mg**	Protein	**9g**	Fiber	**<1g**
Total fat	**11g**				

Smart Tip

When using both the juice and peel of a lime or lemon, grate the peel first, then squeeze the juice. One medium lime will yield about 1½ tablespoons juice and 1½ teaspoons grated peel.

Cool Lime Cheesecake

No-Bake Blueberry Cheesecake

Crust
> **8 zwieback toasts***
> **1 tablespoon butter**

Filling
> **1 envelope (2½ teaspoons) unflavored gelatin**
> **1 cup boiling water**
> **2 packages (8 ounces each) cream cheese, softened**
> **⅓ cup sucralose-based sugar substitute**
> **1 teaspoon vanilla**
> **1 cup thawed frozen whipped topping**
> **¾ cup unsweetened frozen blueberries**

*Zwieback toast can be found in the baby food aisle of most grocery stores.

1. For crust, place zwieback toasts and 1 tablespoon butter in food processor; pulse until coarse crumbs form. Pat thin layer of crumbs on bottom of 9-inch springform pan.

2. Place gelatin in medium bowl. Add boiling water; stir until gelatin is completely dissolved.

3. Beat cream cheese, sugar substitute and vanilla in large bowl at medium speed of electric mixer until well blended. Beat in whipped topping. Add dissolved gelatin in steady stream while beating at low speed. (Mixture will become loose and lumpy.) Beat 4 minutes at medium speed until smooth and creamy, scraping side of bowl occasionally.

4. Fold frozen blueberries into cream cheese mixture; spread in prepared pan. Refrigerate 3 hours or until set. *Makes 8 servings*

Nutrients Per Serving					
Calories	**284**	Cholesterol	**66mg**	Carbohydrate	**11g**
Sodium	**196mg**	Protein	**6g**	Fiber	**1g**
Total fat	**24g**				

No-Bake Blueberry Cheesecake

Baked Desserts

Easy Fruit Tarts

12 wonton skins
Vegetable cooking spray
2 tablespoons apple jelly or apricot fruit spread
1½ cups sliced or cut-up fruit such as DOLE® Bananas, Strawberries or Red or Green Seedless Grapes
1 cup nonfat or low fat yogurt, any flavor

• Press wonton skins into 12 muffin cups sprayed with vegetable cooking spray, allowing corners to stand up over edges of muffin cups.

• Bake at 375°F 5 minutes or until lightly browned. Carefully remove wonton cups to wire rack; cool.

• Cook and stir jelly in small saucepan over low heat until jelly melts.

• Brush bottoms of cooled wonton cups with melted jelly. Place two fruit slices in each cup; spoon rounded tablespoon of yogurt on top of fruit. Garnish with fruit slice and mint leaves. Serve immediately.

Makes 12 servings

Prep Time: 20 minutes
Bake Time: 5 minutes

Nutrients Per Serving (1 tart)					
Calories	**57**	Cholesterol	**2mg**	Carbohydrate	**12g**
Sodium	**32mg**	Protein	**1g**	Fiber	**1g**
Total fat	**<1g**				

Easy Fruit Tarts

Apricot Dessert Soufflé

3 tablespoons butter
2 tablespoons all-purpose flour
1 cup no-sugar-added apricot pourable fruit*
⅓ cup finely chopped dried apricots
3 egg yolks, beaten
4 egg whites
¼ teaspoon cream of tartar
⅛ teaspoon salt

*¾ cup no-sugar-added fruit spread mixed with ¼ cup warm water can be substituted.

Preheat oven to 325°F. Melt butter in medium saucepan. Add flour; cook, stirring constantly, until bubbly. Add pourable fruit and apricots; cook, stirring constantly, until thickened, about 3 minutes. Remove from heat; blend in egg yolks. Cool to room temperature, stirring occasionally. Beat egg whites with cream of tartar and salt at high speed in small bowl of electric mixer until stiff peaks form. Gently fold into apricot mixture. Spoon into 1½-quart soufflé dish. Bake 30 minutes or until puffed and golden brown.** Serve immediately.

Makes 6 servings

**Soufflé will be soft in center. For a firmer soufflé, increase baking time to 35 minutes.

Nutrients Per Serving					
Calories	148	Cholesterol	123mg	Carbohydrate	14g
Sodium	151mg	Protein	4g	Fiber	1g
Total fat	9g				

Apricot Dessert Soufflé

Almond Flour Pound Cake

½ cup (1 stick) butter, softened
½ cup cream cheese, softened
¾ cup sucralose-based sugar substitute
2 tablespoons brown sugar
4 eggs
1 teaspoon vanilla
2 cups almond flour*
1 teaspoon baking powder
½ teaspoon salt
¼ teaspoon ground ginger
¼ teaspoon ground cardamom
1 tablespoon honey roasted sliced almonds
Berries and whipped cream (optional)

Almond flour, also called almond meal, is available at natural foods stores and in the specialty flour section at many supermarkets.

1. Preheat oven to 350°F. Spray 9×5-inch loaf pan (or two mini loaf pans) with nonstick cooking spray.

2. Beat butter, cream cheese, sugar substitute and brown sugar in large bowl with electric mixer until well blended.

3. Add eggs, one at a time, beating after each addition. Beat in vanilla.

4. Combine almond flour with salt, baking powder, ginger and cardamom in medium bowl. Gradually add to egg mixture while beating on medium speed.

5. Pour into prepared pan; sprinkle with honey-roasted almonds. Bake 45 to 55 minutes or until toothpick inserted into center comes out clean. Serve with berries and whipped cream, if desired.

Makes 9 (1-inch) slices

Nutrients Per Serving 1 (1-inch) slice					
Calories	300	Cholesterol	137mg	Carbohydrate	13g
Sodium	517mg	Protein	14g	Fiber	<1g
Total fat	23g				

Almond Flour Pound Cake

Key Lime Tarts

¾ cup fat-free (skim) milk
6 tablespoons fresh lime juice
2 tablespoons cornstarch
½ cup cholesterol-free egg substitute
½ cup reduced-fat sour cream
12 packages sugar substitute *or* equivalent of ½ cup sugar
4 sheets phyllo dough*
Butter-flavored nonstick cooking spray
¾ cup thawed frozen fat-free nondairy whipped topping
Fresh raspberries (optional)

Cover with damp kitchen towel to prevent dough from drying out.

1. Combine milk, lime juice and cornstarch in medium saucepan. Cook over medium heat 2 to 3 minutes, stirring constantly until thick. Remove from heat.

2. Add egg substitute; whisk constantly for 30 seconds to allow egg substitute to cook. Stir in sour cream and sugar substitute; cover and refrigerate until cool.

3. Preheat oven to 350°F. Spray 8 (2½-inch) muffin cups with cooking spray; set aside.

4. Place 1 sheet of phyllo dough on cutting board; spray with cooking spray. Top with second sheet of phyllo dough; spray with cooking spray. Top with third sheet of phyllo dough; spray with cooking spray. Top with last sheet; spray with cooking spray.

5. Cut stack of phyllo dough into 8 squares. Gently fit each stacked square into prepared muffin cup; press firmly against bottom and side. Bake 8 to 10 minutes or until golden brown. Carefully remove from muffin cups; cool on wire rack.

6. Divide lime mixture evenly among phyllo cups; top with whipped topping. Garnish with fresh raspberries, if desired.

Makes 8 servings

Nutrients Per Serving (1 tart)					
Calories	82	Cholesterol	5mg	Carbohydrate	13g
Sodium	88mg	Protein	3g	Fiber	<1g
Total fat	1g				

Key Lime Tarts

Raspberry Cheese Tarts

Crust
1¼ cups graham cracker crumbs
5 tablespoons light margarine (50% less fat and calories)
¼ cup SPLENDA® Granular

Filling
4 ounces reduced-fat cream cheese
½ cup plain nonfat yogurt
1 cup SPLENDA® Granular
½ cup egg substitute
1 cup frozen raspberries

Crust

1. Preheat oven to 350°F. In medium bowl, mix graham cracker crumbs, margarine and ¼ cup SPLENDA®. Press about 1 tablespoon crust mixture into each of 10 muffin pan cups lined with paper liners. Set aside.

Filling

2. In small bowl, beat cream cheese with electric mixer on low speed until soft, about 30 seconds. Add yogurt and beat on low speed until smooth, about 1 minute. Stir in 1 cup SPLENDA® and egg substitute until well blended.

3. Place 1½ tablespoons raspberries (4 to 5) in each muffin cup. Divide filling evenly among muffin cups. Bake for 20 minutes or until firm.

4. Refrigerate for 2 hours before serving. Garnish as desired.

Makes 10 servings

Prep Time: 25 minutes
Bake Time: 20 minutes
Chill Time: 2 hours

Nutrients Per Serving (1 tart)					
Calories	140	Cholesterol	6mg	Carbohydrate	15g
Sodium	255mg	Protein	5g	Fiber	1g
Total fat	6g				

Raspberry Cheese Tarts

Peach Custard

½ **cup peeled fresh peach or nectarine cut into chunks**
1 **can (5 ounces) evaporated fat-free milk***
¼ **cup cholesterol-free egg substitute**
1 **packet sugar substitute** *or* **equivalent of 2 teaspoons sugar**
½ **teaspoon vanilla**
   Cinnamon

*If a 5-ounce can is not available, use ½ cup plus 2 tablespoons evaporated fat-free milk.

1. Preheat oven to 325°F. Divide peach chunks between two 6-ounce ovenproof custard cups. Whisk together milk, egg substitute, sugar substitute and vanilla. Pour mixture over peach chunks in custard cups.

2. Place custard cups in shallow 1-quart casserole. Carefully pour hot water into casserole to depth of 1-inch. Bake custards 50 minutes or until knife inserted in center comes out clean. Remove custard cups from water bath. Serve warm or at room temperature; sprinkle with cinnamon.   *Makes 2 servings*

Note: Drained canned peach slices in juice may be substituted for fresh fruit.

Nutrients Per Serving					
Calories	52	Cholesterol	<1mg	Carbohydrate	7g
Sodium	71mg	Protein	5g	Fiber	1g
Total fat	<1g				

Smart Tip

Store firm peaches at room temperature
in a loosely closed paper bag until they
yield to gentle palm pressure. Once ripe,
use them immediately or refrigerate
them for several days.

Apple Raisin Oatmeal Cookies

1¼ cups EQUAL® SPOONFUL*
1 cup unsweetened applesauce**
½ cup firmly packed brown sugar
6 tablespoons stick butter or margarine, softened
⅓ cup 2% milk
1 egg
2 teaspoons vanilla
2 cups all-purpose flour
1 teaspoon baking soda
1 teaspoon ground cinnamon
¼ teaspoon ground nutmeg
¼ teaspoon salt
1½ cups quick oats, uncooked
1 cup raisins

Can substitute 30 packets EQUAL® sweetener.

**Apple butter can be substituted for the unsweetened applesauce.*

• Combine Equal®, applesauce, brown sugar, butter, milk, egg and vanilla. Mix with electric mixer until well blended. Stir in combined flour, baking soda, cinnamon, nutmeg and salt. Gradually mix in oats and raisins until well combined.

• Drop by tablespoonfuls onto baking sheets lightly sprayed with nonstick cooking spray. Bake in preheated 350°F oven 10 to 12 minutes. Remove from baking sheets and cool completely on wire racks.

Makes about 4 dozen cookies

Nutrients Per Serving (1 cookie)					
Calories	64	Cholesterol	8mg	Carbohydrate	11g
Sodium	57mg	Protein	1g	Fiber	1g
Total fat	2g				

No-Bake Desserts

White Chocolate Pudding Parfaits

> 1 package (4-serving size) sugar-free instant white chocolate pudding mix
> 2 cups (low-fat) 2% milk
> ¾ cup whipping cream
> 1½ cups fresh raspberries or sliced strawberries
> 2 tablespoons chopped roasted shelled pistachio nuts or chopped toasted macadamia nuts

1. Add pudding mix to milk; beat with wire whisk or electric mixer 2 minutes. Refrigerate 5 minutes or until thickened. Beat whipping cream in small deep bowl with electric mixer at high speed until stiff peaks form. Fold whipped cream into pudding.

2. In each of 4 parfait or wine glasses, layer ¼ cup pudding and 2 tablespoons raspberries. Repeat layers. Spoon remaining pudding over berries. Serve immediately or cover and chill up to 6 hours before serving. Just before serving, sprinkle with nuts. *Makes 4 servings*

Nutrients Per Serving					
Calories	**284**	Cholesterol	**71mg**	Carbohydrate	**19g**
Sodium	**291mg**	Protein	**7g**	Fiber	**4g**
Total fat	**21g**				

White Chocolate Pudding Parfaits

Chocolate-Caramel S'Mores

12 chocolate wafer cookies or chocolate graham cracker squares
2 tablespoons fat-free caramel topping
6 large marshmallows

1. Prepare coals for grilling. Place 6 wafer cookies top sides down on plate. Spread 1 teaspoon caramel topping in center of each wafer to within about ¼ inch of edge.

2. Spear 1 to 2 marshmallows onto long wood-handled skewer.* Hold several inches above coals 3 to 5 minutes or until marshmallows are golden and very soft, turning slowly. Push 1 marshmallow off into center of caramel. Top with plain wafer. Repeat with remaining marshmallows and wafers.   *Makes 6 servings*

If wood-handled skewers are unavailable, use oven mitt to protect hand from heat.

Nutrients Per Serving (1 s'more)					
Calories	**72**	Cholesterol	**0mg**	Carbohydrate	**14g**
Sodium	**77mg**	Protein	**1g**	Fiber	**0g**
Total fat	**2g**				

Chocolate-Peanut Butter-Apple Treats

½ (8-ounce package) fat-free or reduced-fat cream cheese, softened
¼ cup reduced-fat chunky peanut butter
2 tablespoons mini chocolate chips
2 large apples

1. Combine cream cheese, peanut butter and chocolate chips in small bowl; mix well.

2. Cut each apple into 12 wedges; discard stems and seeds. Spread about 1½ teaspoons of the mixture over each apple wedge.

Makes 6 servings

Nutrients Per Serving					
Calories	**101**	Cholesterol	**2mg**	Carbohydrate	**12g**
Sodium	**144mg**	Protein	**4g**	Fiber	**2g**
Total fat	**4g**				

Chocolate-Caramel S'Mores

Strawberry Bavarian Deluxe

½ **bag whole frozen unsweetened strawberries**
    (1 mounded quart), partially thawed
¼ **cup low-sugar strawberry preserves**
¼ **cup granular sucralose**
¾ **cup water, divided**
 2 **tablespoons balsamic vinegar**
 2 **envelopes (7g each) unflavored gelatin**
 1 **tablespoon honey**
½ **cup pasteurized liquid egg whites**
½ **teaspoon cream of tartar**
 1 **teaspoon vanilla**
 1 **pint strawberries, washed, dried and hulled**
    Mint sprigs (optional)
 1 **cup thawed frozen light whipped topping**

1. Place frozen strawberries, preserves and sucralose in bowl of food processor fitted with metal blade. Process until smooth. Transfer mixture to bowl. Set aside.

2. Combine ¼ cup water and vinegar in small saucepan. Sprinkle in gelatin and let stand until softened. Add remaining ½ cup water to saucepan with honey; stir to blend. Cook and stir over medium heat until gelatin dissolves.

3. Whisk gelatin mixture into berry mixture in bowl. Refrigerate, covered, until mixture is soupy, but not set.

4. Meanwhile, combine liquid egg whites and cream of tartar in bowl. When berry-gelatin mixture is soupy, whip egg white mixture and vanilla until tripled in volume and at soft peak stage.

5. Gently fold egg whites, ⅓ at a time, into chilled berry-gelatin mixture, being careful not to deflate egg whites. Fold until mixture is uniform color. Scrape mixture into prechilled 2-quart mold, such as a nonstick Bundt pan. Cover and refrigerate at least 8 hours or overnight.

6. To serve, run tip of knife around top of mold, inside rim and center (if using Bundt pan). Dip mold briefly into large bowl of hot water to loosen mousse, lifting occasionally and shaking gently to see if mousse is released. To unmold, center flat serving plate on top of mold, hold firmly so mold doesn't shift, and invert plate and mold. Shake gently to release.

continued on page 40

Strawberry Bavarian Deluxe

Strawberry Bavarian Deluxe, continued

Remove mold and refrigerate. After 10 to 15 minutes, remove from refrigerator and garnish with fresh strawberries and mint sprigs, if desired. Cut into wedges and serve with whipped topping.

Makes 10 servings

Nutrients Per Serving					
Calories	**82**	Cholesterol	**0mg**	Carbohydrate	**15g**
Sodium	**25mg**	Protein	**3g**	Fiber	**2g**
Total fat	**1g**				

Tapioca Pudding

  2¾ **cups low-fat milk**
   ½ **cup SPLENDA® Granular**
   ¼ **cup egg substitute**
   3 **tablespoons quick-cooking tapioca**
   ⅛ **teaspoon salt**
  1½ **teaspoons vanilla**

1. In large saucepan, combine milk, SPLENDA®, egg substitute, tapioca and salt. Stir until blended, about 30 seconds. Let stand for 5 minutes.

2. Heat over medium heat, stirring constantly, until pudding comes to a full boil.

3. Remove from heat and stir in vanilla. Cool at room temperature for 20 minutes. Stir once and serve.

Makes 6 servings

Prep Time: 25 minutes
Cook Time: 15 minutes

Nutrients Per Serving (½ cup)					
Calories	**92**	Cholesterol	**9mg**	Carbohydrate	**12g**
Sodium	**125mg**	Protein	**5g**	Fiber	**<1g**
Total fat	**2g**				

Coconut Flan

3 tablespoons water
1 envelope (2½ teaspoons) unflavored gelatin
1 can (14½ ounces) unsweetened coconut milk
8 packets sucralose-based sugar substitute
2 tablespoons powdered sugar
½ teaspoon vanilla
4 tablespoons toasted flaked coconut
2 slices (½ inch thick) fresh pineapple, cut into pieces

1. Place water in small bowl and sprinkle with gelatin; set aside.

2. Place coconut milk, sugar substitute, powdered sugar and vanilla in medium saucepan. Heat over medium heat; stir to dissolve sugar and smooth out coconut milk. *Do not boil.* Add gelatin mixture; stir until gelatin is completely dissolved.

3. Pour coconut milk mixture evenly into four 5-ounce custard cups. Refrigerate about 3 hours or until set.

4. To unmold, run knife around outside edges of cups; place cups in hot water about 30 seconds. Place serving plate over cup; invert and shake until flan drops onto plate. Top each serving with 1 tablespoon toasted coconut and ¼ of pineapple pieces. Refrigerate leftovers.

Makes 4 servings

Note: Flan is best eaten within 2 days.

Nutrients Per Serving					
Calories	**261**	Cholesterol	**0mg**	Carbohydrate	**13g**
Sodium	**18mg**	Protein	**4g**	Fiber	**1g**
Total fat	**24g**				

Pineapple-Ginger Bavarian

1 can (8 ounces) crushed pineapple in juice, drained and liquid reserved
1 package (4-serving size) sugar-free orange gelatin
1 cup sugar-free ginger ale
1 cup plain nonfat yogurt
¾ teaspoon grated fresh ginger
½ cup whipping cream
1 packet sugar substitute
¼ teaspoon vanilla

1. Combine reserved pineapple juice with enough water to equal ½ cup liquid. Pour into small saucepan. Bring to a boil over high heat.

2. Place gelatin in medium bowl. Add pineapple juice mixture; stir until gelatin is completely dissolved. Add ginger ale and half of crushed pineapple; stir until well blended. Add yogurt; whisk until well blended. Pour into 5 individual ramekins. Cover each ramekin with plastic wrap; refrigerate until firm.

3. Meanwhile, combine remaining half of pineapple with ginger in small bowl. Cover with plastic wrap; refrigerate.

4. Just before serving, beat cream in small deep bowl on high speed of electric mixer until soft peaks form. Add sugar substitute and vanilla; beat until stiff peaks form.

5. To serve, top bavarian with 1 tablespoon whipped topping and 1 tablespoon pineapple mixture. *Makes 5 servings*

Tip: To save time, use 2 tablespoons ready-made whipped topping to garnish.

Nutrients Per Serving					
Calories	**147**	Cholesterol	**34mg**	Carbohydrate	**12g**
Sodium	**102mg**	Protein	**4g**	Fiber	**<1g**
Total fat	**9g**				

Pineapple-Ginger Bavarian

Sparkling Strawberry-Lime Shake

2 cups (10 ounces) frozen whole unsweetened strawberries
1¼ cups lime-flavored sparkling water, divided
¼ cup whipping cream or half-and-half
1 tablespoon sugar substitute
Lime wedges or slices

1. Place strawberries in blender container; allow to thaw 5 minutes before proceeding. Add 1 cup sparkling water, cream and sugar substitute. Cover; blend until smooth, scraping down side of blender once or twice (mixture will be thick).

2. Gently stir in remaining sparkling water; pour into 2 glasses. Garnish with lime wedges. *Makes 2 servings*

Variations: For a tropical variation, add 1 teaspoon banana extract and/or ½ teaspoon coconut extract along with the cream. For a rum-flavored drink, add ½ teaspoon rum extract.

Tip: For quick shakes any time, wash, hull and freeze whole strawberries in a tightly covered container.

Nutrients Per Serving					
Calories	**156**	Cholesterol	**41mg**	Carbohydrate	**15g**
Sodium	**18mg**	Protein	**2g**	Fiber	**2g**
Total fat	**12g**				

Smart Tip

Surprisingly, whipping cream contains
fewer carbs than half-and-half. However,
both are high in fat and should only
be used in moderation.

Sparkling Strawberry-Lime Shake

Fresh Strawberry Cream Pie

1 quart fresh medium strawberries
1 tablespoon EQUAL® SPOONFUL*
    Pastry for single-crust 9-inch pie, baked
1 package (8 ounces) reduced-fat cream cheese, softened
⅓ cup vanilla-flavored light nonfat yogurt
¼ cup EQUAL® SPOONFUL**
1 tablespoon lemon juice

May substitute 1½ packets Equal® sweetener.

**May substitute 6 packets Equal® sweetener.*

• Remove stems from several strawberries and slice to make 1 cup. Toss with 1 tablespoon Equal® Spoonful. Spread on bottom of baked pie shell.

• Beat cream cheese, yogurt, ¼ cup Equal® Spoonful and lemon juice until smooth and fluffy. Spread over sliced strawberries in pie shell. Remove stems from all but 1 large strawberry. Cut berries lengthwise in half. Place, cut side down, over cream cheese mixture, around outer edge of pie crust, with pointed end of berry facing center of pie. Make several thin slits in last whole berry starting near top and going to pointed end. Press gently with fingers to form "fan". Place in center of pie.

• Refrigerate pie at least 4 hours before serving.   *Makes 8 servings*

Nutrients Per Serving					
Calories	**185**	Cholesterol	**20mg**	Carbohydrate	**13g**
Sodium	**144mg**	Protein	**4g**	Fiber	**2g**
Total fat	**9g**				

Fresh Strawberry Cream Pie

Three-Melon Soup

3 cups cubed seeded watermelon
3 tablespoons unsweetened pineapple juice
2 tablespoons lemon juice
¼ cantaloupe melon
⅛ honeydew melon

1. Combine watermelon, pineapple juice and lemon juice in blender; blend until smooth. Chill at least 2 hours or overnight.

2. Scoop out balls of cantaloupe and honeydew.

3. To serve, pour watermelon mixture into shallow bowls; garnish with cantaloupe and honeydew.

Makes 4 servings

Nutrients Per Serving					
Calories	**68**	Cholesterol	**0mg**	Carbohydrate	**16g**
Sodium	**9mg**	Protein	**1g**	Fiber	**1g**
Total fat	**1g**				

Smart Tip

A ripe watermelon will have a shrunken and discolored stem and will produce a hollow sound when thumped with your knuckles. When choosing cut watermelon, look for bright-colored flesh with black seeds. The end nearest the stem is usually the sweetest. Avoid cut melon with coarse pale flesh, dark wet-looking flesh (overripe) or an abundance of small white seeds (underripe).

Three-Melon Soup

Lighter Than Air Chocolate Delight

2 envelopes unflavored gelatin
½ cup cold water
1 cup boiling water
1⅓ cups nonfat dry milk powder
⅓ cup HERSHEY'S Cocoa or HERSHEY'S Dutch Processed Cocoa
1 tablespoon vanilla extract
Dash salt
Granulated sugar substitute to equal 14 teaspoons sugar
8 large ice cubes

1. Sprinkle gelatin over cold water in blender container; let stand 4 minutes to soften. Gently stir with rubber spatula, scraping gelatin particles off sides; add boiling water to gelatin mixture. Cover; blend until gelatin dissolves. Add milk powder, cocoa, vanilla and salt; blend on medium speed until well mixed. Add sugar substitute and ice cubes; blend on high speed until ice is crushed and mixture is smooth and fluffy.

2. Immediately pour into 4-cup mold. Cover; refrigerate until firm. Unmold onto serving plate. *Makes 8 servings*

Note: Eight individual dessert dishes may be used in place of 4-cup mold, if desired.

Nutrients Per Serving					
Calories	**72**	Cholesterol	**2mg**	Carbohydrate	**10g**
Sodium	**67mg**	Protein	**6g**	Fiber	**1g**
Total fat	**<1g**				

Streusel-Topped Strawberry Cheesecake Squares

1 container (8 ounces) strawberry-flavored nonfat yogurt with aspartame sweetener
1 package (8 ounces) fat-free cream cheese
4 ounces reduced-fat cream cheese
6 packets sugar substitute *or* equivalent of ¼ cup sugar
1 packet unflavored gelatin
2 tablespoons water
1 cup fresh chopped strawberries
1 tablespoon sugar
1 cup fresh sliced strawberries
⅓ cup low-fat granola

1. Line 9-inch square baking pan with plastic wrap, leaving 4-inch overhang on 2 opposite sides.

2. Combine yogurt, cream cheese and sugar substitute in medium bowl; beat until smooth. Set aside.

3. Combine gelatin and water in small microwavable bowl; let stand 2 minutes. Microwave at HIGH 40 seconds to dissolve gelatin. Beat gelatin into yogurt mixture. Combine chopped strawberries and sugar in small bowl. Add to yogurt mixture.

4. Pour yogurt mixture into prepared pan; level with spatula. Refrigerate 1 hour or until firm.

5. Just before serving, arrange remaining 1 cup sliced strawberries on top; sprinkle with granola.

6. Gently lift cheesecake out of pan with plastic wrap. Pull plastic wrap away from sides; cut into 9 to 12 squares.   *Makes 9 to 12 servings*

Nutrients Per Serving (1 square)					
Calories	**98**	Cholesterol	**8mg**	Carbohydrate	**11g**
Sodium	**223mg**	Protein	**7g**	Fiber	**1g**
Total fat	**3g**				

Frozen Desserts

Café au Lait Ice Cream Sundae

3 cups whipping cream, divided
4 egg yolks, lightly beaten
1 tablespoon instant coffee granules
½ cup plus 2 tablespoons no-calorie sugar substitute for baking, divided
½ teaspoon vanilla
½ cup chopped walnuts or pecans

1. Pour 2 cups cream into medium saucepan. Whisk egg yolks and coffee granules into cream. Heat 10 minutes over low heat, stirring constantly, until mixture reaches 160°F. Mixture will thicken as it cooks.

2. Pour mixture into bowl; stir in ½ cup sugar substitute until well blended. Refrigerate 2 to 3 hours or until cold. Pour chilled mixture into ice cream maker; process according to manufacturer's directions.

3. Whip remaining 1 cup cream, 2 tablespoons sugar substitute and vanilla until stiff. Scoop ice cream into serving bowls; top with whipped cream. Sprinkle with nuts just before serving.   *Makes 4 servings*

Tip: The ice cream will become harder the longer it is stored in freezer, so it is best eaten when freshly made.

Nutrients Per Serving					
Calories	**798**	Cholesterol	**459mg**	Carbohydrate	**12g**
Sodium	**79mg**	Protein	**9g**	Fiber	**1g**
Total fat	**82g**				

Café au Lait Ice Cream Sundae

Frozen Berry Ice Cream

8 ounces frozen unsweetened strawberries, partially thawed
8 ounces frozen unsweetened peaches, partially thawed
4 ounces frozen unsweetened blueberries, partially thawed
6 packets sugar substitute
2 teaspoons vanilla
2 cups no-sugar-added light vanilla ice cream
16 blueberries
4 small strawberries, halved
8 peach slices

In food processor, combine frozen strawberries, peaches, blueberries, sugar substitute and vanilla. Process until coarsely chopped. Add ice cream; process until well blended.

Serve immediately for semi-soft texture or freeze until needed and allow to stand 10 minutes to soften slightly. Garnish each serving with 2 blueberries for "eyes," 1 strawberry half for "nose" and 1 peach slice for "smile." *Makes 8 servings*

Nutrients Per Serving (½ cup)					
Calories	**69**	Cholesterol	**0mg**	Carbohydrate	**15g**
Sodium	**23mg**	Protein	**3g**	Fiber	**1g**
Total fat	**<1g**				

Easy Raspberry Ice Cream

8 ounces (1¾ cups) frozen raspberries (not frozen in syrup or juice)
2 to 3 tablespoons powdered sugar
½ cup whipping cream

Pulse raspberries in food processor about 15 seconds or until they resemble coarse crumbs. Add sugar; pulse about 5 seconds more or until well blended. With machine running, slowly add cream; process about 10 seconds or until well blended and raspberries have lightened in color. Serve immediately. *Makes 3 servings*

Nutrients Per Serving (½ cup)					
Calories	**193**	Cholesterol	**54mg**	Carbohydrate	**15g**
Sodium	**15mg**	Protein	**2g**	Fiber	**3g**
Total fat	**15g**				

Frozen Berry Ice Cream

Speedy Pineapple-Lime Sorbet

1 ripe pineapple, cut into cubes (about 4 cups)
⅓ cup frozen limeade concentrate, thawed
1 to 2 tablespoons fresh lime juice
1 teaspoon grated lime peel

1. Arrange pineapple in single layer on large sheet pan; freeze at least 1 hour or until very firm. Use metal spatula to transfer pineapple to resealable plastic freezer food storage bags; freeze up to 1 month.

2. Combine pineapple, limeade, lime juice and lime peel in food processor; process until smooth and fluffy. If pineapple doesn't become smooth and fluffy, let stand 30 minutes to soften slightly; then repeat processing. Serve immediately.   *Makes 8 servings*

Note: This dessert is best if served immediately, but it may be made ahead, stored in the freezer and then softened several minutes before serving.

Nutrients Per Serving (½ cup)					
Calories	**56**	Cholesterol	**0mg**	Carbohydrate	**15g**
Sodium	**1mg**	Protein	**<1g**	Fiber	**1g**
Total fat	**<1g**				

Smart Tip

When selecting a fresh pineapple, choose one that is heavy for its size. Look for crown leaves that are dark green and fresh looking. Also, sniff the pineapple—a fragrant pineapple aroma is a good sign of ripeness. Avoid pineapples that are green, have soft spots, dry-looking leaves or a fermented aroma.

Speedy Pineapple-Lime Sorbet

Watermelon Ice

4 **cups seeded 1-inch watermelon chunks**
¼ cup thawed frozen unsweetened pineapple juice concentrate
2 **tablespoons fresh lime juice**
   Fresh melon balls (optional)
   Fresh mint leaves (optional)

Place melon chunks in single layer in plastic freezer bag; freeze until firm, about 8 hours. Place frozen melon in food processor container fitted with steel blade. Let stand 15 minutes to soften slightly. Add pineapple juice and lime juice. Remove plunger from top of food processor to allow air to be incorporated. Process until smooth, scraping down side of container frequently. Spoon into individual dessert dishes. Garnish with melon balls and mint leaves, if desired. Freeze leftovers.   *Makes 6 servings*

Honeydew Ice: Substitute honeydew for watermelon and unsweetened pineapple-guava-orange juice concentrate for pineapple juice concentrate.

Cantaloupe Ice: Substitute cantaloupe for watermelon and unsweetened pineapple-guava-orange juice concentrate for pineapple juice concentrate.

Note: Ices may be transferred to airtight container and frozen up to 1 month. Let stand at room temperature 10 minutes to soften slightly before serving.

Nutrients Per Serving					
Calories	57	Cholesterol	0mg	Carbohydrate	13g
Sodium	3mg	Protein	1g	Fiber	1g
Total fat	<1g				

Watermelon Ice, Honeydew Ice and Cantaloupe Ice

Cherry-Peach Pops

⅓ cup peach nectar or apricot nectar
1 teaspoon unflavored gelatin
1 (15-ounce) can sliced peaches in light syrup, drained
1 (6- or 8-ounce) carton fat-free, sugar-free peach or cherry yogurt
1 (6- or 8-ounce) carton fat-free, sugar-free cherry yogurt

1. Combine nectar and unflavored gelatin in small saucepan; let stand 5 minutes. Heat and stir over low heat just until gelatin dissolves.

2. Combine nectar mixture, drained peaches and yogurt in food processor. Cover and process until smooth.

3. Pour into 7 (3-ounce) paper cups, filling each about ⅔ full. Place in freezer; freeze 1 hour. Insert wooden stick into center of each cup. Freeze at least 3 more hours.

4. Let stand at room temperature 10 minutes before serving. Tear away paper cups to serve.

Makes 7 servings

Nutrients Per Serving (1 pop)					
Calories	**52**	Cholesterol	**1mg**	Carbohydrate	**11g**
Sodium	**34mg**	Protein	**2g**	Fiber	**<1g**
Total fat	**<1g**				

Tempting Chocolate Mousse

1 envelope unflavored gelatin
2½ cups nonfat milk
¼ cup HERSHEY'S Cocoa or HERSHEY'S Dutch Processed Cocoa
1 tablespoon cornstarch
1 egg yolk
1 teaspoon vanilla extract
Granulated sugar substitute to equal 8 teaspoons sugar
1 cup prepared sucrose-free whipped topping*

*Prepare 1 envelope (1 ounce) sucrose-free dry whipped topping mix with ½ cup very cold water according to package directions. (This makes about 2 cups topping; use 1 cup topping for mousse. Reserve remainder for garnishing, if desired.)

1. Sprinkle gelatin over milk in medium saucepan; let stand 5 minutes to soften. Stir in cocoa, cornstarch and egg yolk; cook over medium heat, stirring constantly with whisk, until mixture comes to a boil. Reduce heat to low; cook, stirring constantly, until mixture thickens slightly, about 1 minute.

2. Remove from heat; cool to lukewarm. Stir in vanilla and sugar substitute. Pour mixture into medium bowl. Refrigerate, stirring occasionally, until thickened, about 45 minutes.

3. Fold 1 cup prepared whipped topping into chocolate mixture. Spoon into 6 individual dessert dishes. Cover; refrigerate until firm. Garnish with remaining whipped topping, if desired.

Makes 6 servings

Nutrients Per Serving					
Calories	**90**	Cholesterol	**35mg**	Carbohydrate	**11g**
Sodium	**55mg**	Protein	**9g**	Fiber	**0g**
Total fat	**3g**				

Irresistible Cookies

Chocolate Chip Cookies

⅓ cup stick butter or margarine, softened
1 egg
1 teaspoon vanilla
⅓ cup EQUAL® SPOONFUL*
⅓ cup firmly packed light brown sugar
¾ cup all-purpose flour
½ teaspoon baking soda
¼ teaspoon salt
½ cup semi-sweet chocolate chips or mini chocolate chips

*May substitute 8 packets Equal® sweetener.

• Beat butter with electric mixer until fluffy. Beat in egg and vanilla until blended. Mix in Equal® and brown sugar until combined.

• Combine flour, baking soda and salt. Mix into butter mixture until well blended. Stir in chocolate chips.

• Drop dough by rounded teaspoonfuls onto ungreased baking sheet. Bake in preheated 350°F oven 8 to 10 minutes or until light golden color. Remove from baking sheet and cool completely on wire rack.

Makes about 2 dozen cookies

Nutrients Per Serving (1 cookie)					
Calories	67	Cholesterol	16mg	Carbohydrate	8g
Sodium	80mg	Protein	1g	Fiber	<1g
Total fat	4g				

Chocolate Chip Cookies

Peanut Butter Granola Bites

2 cups cornflakes cereal
1 cup quick oats, uncooked
⅔ cup seedless raisins
½ cup chunky peanut butter
½ cup egg substitute *or* 4 egg whites
1 cup EQUAL® SPOONFUL*
1 tablespoon honey
2 teaspoons vanilla
1 teaspoon ground cinnamon

*May substitute 24 packets EQUAL® sweetener.

• Combine cornflakes, oats and raisins in large bowl.

• Combine peanut butter and egg substitute in medium bowl. Stir in Equal®, honey, vanilla and cinnamon until well blended. Spoon over cereal mixture. Toss gently to combine. Let stand 5 minutes.

• Preheat oven to 350°F. Shape mixture into 1-inch balls. Place on lightly sprayed baking sheet. Bake 8 to 10 minutes or until lightly golden and set. Remove to wire racks to cool completely.

Makes about 2½ dozen

Nutrients Per Serving (1 cookie)					
Calories	61	Cholesterol	0mg	Carbohydrate	9g
Sodium	42mg	Protein	2g	Fiber	<1g
Total fat	2g				

Thumbprint Cookies

6 tablespoons stick butter or margarine
1 cup EQUAL® SPOONFUL*
1 egg
2 tablespoons 2% milk
1 teaspoon vanilla
1¼ cups all-purpose flour
¼ teaspoon baking powder
¼ teaspoon baking soda
¼ teaspoon salt
¾ cup sugar-free preserves or spreadable fruit of choice

May substitute 24 packets EQUAL® sweetener.

• Beat butter and Equal® until well combined. Mix in egg, milk and vanilla until blended. Gradually beat in combined flour, baking powder, baking soda and salt.

• Shape dough by teaspoonfuls into balls. Place on baking sheets sprayed with nonstick cooking spary. Press thumb deeply into dough to form "thumbprint" indentation. Bake in preheated 350°F oven 11 to 13 minutes. Remove from baking sheets and cool completely on wire rack. Fill each cookie with about ½ teaspoon preserves just before serving.   *Makes about 2 dozen cookies*

Nutrients Per Serving (1 cookie)					
Calories	**70**	Cholesterol	**17mg**	Carbohydrate	**9g**
Sodium	**67mg**	Protein	**1g**	Fiber	**<1g**
Total fat	**3g**				

Apple-Cranberry Crescent Cookies

1¼ cups chopped apples
½ cup dried cranberries
½ cup reduced-fat sour cream
¼ cup cholesterol-free egg substitute
¼ cup margarine or butter, melted
3 tablespoons sugar, divided
1 package quick-rise active dry yeast
1 teaspoon vanilla
2 cups all-purpose flour
1 teaspoon ground cinnamon
1 tablespoon reduced-fat (2%) milk

1. Preheat oven to 350°F. Lightly coat cookie sheet with nonstick cooking spray.

2. Place apples and cranberries in food processor or blender; pulse to finely chop. Set aside.

3. Combine sour cream, egg substitute, margarine and 2 tablespoons sugar in medium bowl. Add yeast and vanilla. Add flour; stir to form ball. Turn dough out onto lightly floured work surface. Knead 1 minute. Cover with plastic wrap; allow to stand 10 minutes.

4. Divide dough into thirds. Roll one portion into 12-inch circle. Spread with ⅓ apple mixture (about ¼ cup). Cut dough to make 8 wedges. Roll up each wedge, beginning at outside edge. Place on prepared cookie sheet; turn ends of cookies to form crescents. Repeat with remaining dough and apple mixture.

5. Combine remaining 1 tablespoon sugar and cinnamon in small bowl. Lightly brush cookies with milk; sprinkle with sugar-cinnamon mixture. Bake cookies 18 to 20 minutes or until lightly browned.

Makes 2 dozen cookies

Nutrients Per Serving (1 cookie)					
Calories	**82**	Cholesterol	**2mg**	Carbohydrate	**13g**
Sodium	**31mg**	Protein	**2g**	Fiber	**1g**
Total fat	**2g**				

Apple-Cranberry Crescent Cookies

Pumpkin Polka Dot Cookies

1¼ cups EQUAL® SPOONFUL*
½ cup stick butter or margarine, softened
3 tablespoons light molasses
1 cup canned pumpkin
1 egg
1½ teaspoons vanilla
1⅔ cups all-purpose flour
1 teaspoon baking powder
1¼ teaspoons ground cinnamon
½ teaspoon ground nutmeg
½ teaspoon ground ginger
½ teaspoon baking soda
¼ teaspoon salt
1 cup mini semi-sweet chocolate chips

May substitute 30 packets Equal® sweetener.

• Beat Equal®, butter and molasses until well combined. Mix in pumpkin, egg and vanilla until blended. Gradually stir in combined flour, baking powder, spices, baking soda and salt until well blended. Stir in chocolate chips.

• Drop by teaspoonfuls onto baking sheet sprayed with nonstick cooking spray. Bake in preheated 350°F oven 11 to 13 minutes. Remove from baking sheet and cool completely on wire rack. Store at room temperature in airtight container up to 1 week.

Makes about 4 dozen cookies

Nutrients Per Serving (1 cookie)					
Calories	63	Cholesterol	10mg	Carbohydrate	8g
Sodium	69mg	Protein	1g	Fiber	1g
Total fat	3g				

Pumpkin Polka Dot Cookies

Almond Biscotti

¼ **cup finely chopped slivered almonds**
½ **cup sugar**
2 **tablespoons margarine**
4 **egg whites, lightly beaten**
2 **teaspoons almond extract**
2 **cups all-purpose flour**
2 **teaspoons baking powder**
¼ **teaspoon salt**

1. Preheat oven to 375°F. Place almonds in small baking pan. Bake 7 to 8 minutes or until golden brown.

2. Beat sugar and margarine in medium bowl with electric mixer until smooth. Add egg whites and almond extract; mix well. Combine flour, baking powder and salt in large bowl; mix well. Stir egg white mixture and almonds into flour mixture until well blended.

3. Spray two 9×5-inch loaf pans with nonstick cooking spray. Divide dough between prepared pans; spread evenly onto bottoms of pans with wet fingertips. Bake 15 minutes or until knife inserted into centers comes out clean. Remove from oven; turn out onto cutting board.

4. As soon as loaves are cool enough to handle, cut each loaf into 16 (½-inch-thick) slices. Place slices on baking sheets covered with parchment paper or sprayed with cooking spray. Bake 5 minutes; turn over. Bake 5 minutes more or until golden brown. Serve warm or cool completely and store in airtight container.   *Makes 32 biscotti*

Nutrients Per Serving (1 biscotti)					
Calories	56	Cholesterol	0mg	Carbohydrate	9g
Sodium	53mg	Protein	1g	Fiber	<1g
Total fat	1g				

Almond Biscotti

Chocolate Cannoli

1 cup heavy cream
1 square (1 ounce) unsweetened chocolate
⅔ cup sucralose-based sugar substitute
⅓ cup whole milk ricotta cheese
1 teaspoon vanilla or almond extract
¼ teaspoon salt
8 unfilled cannoli shells (½ ounce each)*
1 teaspoon miniature chocolate chips or crushed pistachio nuts
   (optional)

Cannoli shells can be found at Italian bakeries and delis or in the ethnic food aisles at some supermarkets. If shells are unavailable, serve filling in dessert dish with sugar wafer or other cookie.

1. Beat cream in medium bowl at high speed of electric mixer until stiff peaks form; set aside.

2. Place chocolate in small microwavable bowl; microwave at HIGH 1 to 2 minutes or until chocolate is melted, stirring at 30-second intervals.

3. Combine sugar substitute, ricotta, vanilla and salt in medium bowl. Stir in melted chocolate. Fold whipped cream into mixture.

4. Spoon or pipe ¼ cup mixture into each cannoli shell. Garnish with chocolate chips or crushed pistachio nuts, if desired.

Makes 8 servings

Nutrients Per Serving					
Calories	**230**	Cholesterol	**46mg**	Carbohydrate	**12g**
Sodium	**23mg**	Protein	**3g**	Fiber	**1g**
Total fat	**18g**				

Chocolate Cannoli

Chewy Apple Moons

¾ **cup thawed frozen unsweetened apple juice concentrate**
½ **cup coarsely chopped dried apples**
 2 **eggs**
¼ **cup butter, melted and cooled**
 1 **teaspoon vanilla**
1¼ **cups all-purpose flour**
 ½ **teaspoon baking powder**
 ½ **teaspoon ground cinnamon**
 ¼ **teaspoon salt**
 ⅛ **teaspoon ground nutmeg**

Preheat oven to 350°F. Combine apple juice concentrate and apples; let stand 10 minutes. Beat eggs in medium bowl. Blend in concentrate mixture, butter and vanilla. Add remaining ingredients; mix well. Drop tablespoonfuls of dough 2 inches apart onto greased cookie sheets. Bake 10 to 12 minutes or until firm and golden brown. Cool on wire rack. Store in tightly covered container.   *Makes 1½ dozen cookies*

Nutrients Per Serving (1 cookie)					
Calories	90	Cholesterol	31mg	Carbohydrate	13g
Sodium	86mg	Protein	1g	Fiber	<1g
Total fat	3g				

Little Butterscotch Candy Cookies

½ **cup pourable sucralose sugar substitute***
3 **tablespoons canola oil**
¼ **cup cholesterol-free egg substitute**
2 **tablespoons molasses**
1 **teaspoon vanilla**
1 **cup uncooked old-fashioned oats**
⅓ **cup all-purpose flour**
1½ **teaspoons ground cinnamon**
½ **teaspoon baking soda**
⅛ **teaspoon salt**
½ **cup butterscotch morsels or golden raisins**

*Sucralose-based sugar substitute is sold under the brand name Splenda®.

1. Preheat oven to 375°F.

2. In medium mixing bowl, combine sugar substitute and oil. Using electric mixer, beat until well blended, about 30 seconds (mixture will resemble small peas). Add egg substitute, molasses and vanilla; blend well. Add remaining ingredients, except butterscotch morsels; beat until well blended. Add butterscotch morsels; mix well.

3. Lightly coat two nonstick baking sheets with nonstick cooking spray. Using teaspoon, spoon 20 cookies on each baking sheet. Coat fork with cooking spray and gently flatten each cookie. Bake 2½ minutes for chewy texture or 3 minutes for cake-like texture. Do not overbake (cookies will not look done when removed from oven). Place baking sheet on wire rack and let stand 1 minute; immediately remove cookies from baking sheet and allow to cool completely on wire rack. Cool cookies before serving for best flavor and texture.

Makes 40 cookies

Nutrients Per Serving (2 cookies)					
Calories	**84**	Cholesterol	**<1mg**	Carbohydrate	**10g**
Sodium	**39mg**	Protein	**1g**	Fiber	**<1g**
Total fat	**4g**				

Cocoa Nutty Bites

1 cup creamy unsweetened natural peanut butter*
½ cup light brown sugar, not packed
¼ cup sucralose-based sugar substitute
1 tablespoon unsweetened cocoa powder
½ teaspoon ground cinnamon
¼ teaspoon salt
¼ teaspoon ground ginger
1 egg, beaten

Choose natural peanut butter that is not hydrogenated. Check label carefully.

1. Preheat oven to 350°F. Combine peanut butter, brown sugar, sugar substitute, cocoa, cinnamon, salt and ginger in medium bowl. Add egg; stir until well blended.

2. Shape dough into 24 (1-inch) balls. Place on ungreased cookie sheets. Flatten balls with fork to 1/2-inch thickness.

3. Bake 10 to 12 minutes or until cookies are firm and lightly browned. Cool on cookie sheets 5 minutes. Remove to wire racks; cool completely.

Makes 24 cookies

Note: This simple recipe is unusual because it doesn't contain any flour—but it still makes great cookies!

Nutrients Per Serving (1 cookie)					
Calories	85	Cholesterol	9mg	Carbohydrate	8g
Sodium	79mg	Protein	3g	Fiber	1g
Total fat	5g				

Cocoa Nutty Bites

Chocolate-Almond Meringue Puffs

  2 tablespoons granulated sugar
  3 packages sugar substitute
1½ teaspoons unsweetened cocoa powder
  2 egg whites, at room temperature
  ½ teaspoon vanilla
  ¼ teaspoon cream of tartar
  ¼ teaspoon almond extract
  ⅛ teaspoon salt
1½ ounces sliced almonds
  3 tablespoons sugar-free seedless raspberry fruit spread

1. Preheat oven to 275°F. Combine granulated sugar, sugar substitute and cocoa powder in small bowl; set aside.

2. Beat egg whites in small bowl on high speed of electric mixer until foamy. Add vanilla, cream of tartar, almond extract and salt; beat until soft peaks form. Add sugar mixture, 1 tablespoon at a time, beating until stiff peaks form.

3. Line baking sheet with foil. Spoon 15 equal mounds of egg white mixture onto foil. Sprinkle with almonds.

4. Bake 1 hour. Turn oven off but do not open oven door. Leave puffs in oven 2 hours longer or until completely dry. Remove from oven; cool completely.

5. Stir fruit spread and spoon about ½ teaspoon onto each meringue just before serving. *Makes 15 cookies*

Tip: Cookies are best if eaten the same day they're made. If necessary, store in airtight container, adding fruit topping at time of serving.

Nutrients Per Serving (1 cookie)					
Calories	**34**	Cholesterol	**0mg**	Carbohydrate	**4g**
Sodium	**27mg**	Protein	**1g**	Fiber	**<1g**
Total fat	**1g**				

Chocolate-Almond Meringue Puffs

Peanut Butter & Banana Cookies

¼ **cup butter**
½ **cup mashed ripe banana**
½ **cup no-sugar-added natural peanut butter**
¼ **cup thawed frozen unsweetened apple juice concentrate**
 1 **egg**
 1 **teaspoon vanilla**
 1 **cup all-purpose flour**
½ **teaspoon baking soda**
¼ **teaspoon salt**
½ **cup chopped salted peanuts**
  Whole peanuts (optional)

Preheat oven to 375°F. Beat butter in large bowl until creamy. Add banana and peanut butter; beat until smooth. Blend in apple juice concentrate, egg and vanilla. Beat in flour, baking soda and salt. Stir in chopped peanuts. Drop rounded tablespoonfuls of dough 2 inches apart onto lightly greased cookie sheets; top each with one whole peanut, if desired. Bake 8 minutes or until set. Cool completely on wire racks. Store in tightly covered container.   *Makes 2 dozen cookies*

Nutrients Per Serving (1 cookie)					
Calories	**100**	Cholesterol	**14mg**	Carbohydrate	**9g**
Sodium	**88mg**	Protein	**3g**	Fiber	**1g**
Total fat	**6g**				

Peanut Butter & Banana Cookies

Oatmeal Almond Balls

¼ **cup sliced almonds**
⅓ **cup honey**
 2 **egg whites**
½ **teaspoon ground cinnamon**
⅛ **teaspoon salt**
1½ **cups uncooked quick oats**

1. Preheat oven to 350°F. Place almonds on cookie sheet; bake 8 to 10 minutes or until golden brown. Set aside. Do not turn off oven.

2. Combine honey, egg whites, cinnamon and salt in large bowl; mix well. Add oats and toasted almonds; mix well.

3. Drop by rounded teaspoonfuls onto ungreased nonstick cookie sheet. Bake 12 minutes or until lightly browned. Remove to wire rack to cool.   *Makes 24 servings*

Tip: Store unopened packages of nuts in a cool, dark place. Store opened packages of nuts in an airtight container in the refrigerator for six months, or in the freezer for up to two years.

Nutrients Per Serving (1 cookie)					
Calories	**42**	Cholesterol	**0mg**	Carbohydrate	**7g**
Sodium	**16mg**	Protein	**1g**	Fiber	**0g**
Total fat	**1g**				

Oatmeal Almond Balls

Brownies & Bars

Peanut Butter Chocolate Bars

1 cup EQUAL® SPOONFUL*
½ cup (1 stick) butter or margarine, softened
⅓ cup firmly packed brown sugar
½ cup 2% milk
½ cup creamy peanut butter
1 egg
1 teaspoon vanilla
1 cup all-purpose flour
1 cup quick oats, uncooked
½ teaspoon baking soda
¼ teaspoon salt
¾ cup mini semi-sweet chocolate chips

*May substitute 24 packets Equal® sweetener.

• Beat Equal®, butter and brown sugar until well combined. Stir in milk, peanut butter, egg and vanilla until blended. Gradually mix in combined flour, oats, baking soda and salt until blended. Stir in chocolate chips.

• Spread mixture evenly in 13×9-inch baking pan generously coated with nonstick cooking spray. Bake in preheated 350°F oven 20 to 22 minutes. Cool completely in pan on wire rack. Cut into squares; store in airtight container at room temperature.   *Makes 48 bars*

Nutrients Per Serving (1 bar)					
Calories	75	Cholesterol	10mg	Carbohydrate	8g
Sodium	60mg	Protein	1g	Fiber	1g
Total fat	5g				

Peanut Butter Chocolate Bars

Lemon-Cranberry Bars

½ **cup frozen lemonade concentrate, thawed**
½ **cup sugar substitute**
¼ **cup margarine**
1 **egg**
1½ **cups all-purpose flour**
2 **teaspoons grated lemon peel**
½ **teaspoon baking soda**
½ **teaspoon salt**
½ **cup dried cranberries**

1. Preheat oven to 375°F. Lightly coat 8-inch square baking pan with nonstick cooking spray; set aside.

2. Combine lemonade concentrate, sugar substitute, margarine and egg in medium bowl; mix well. Add flour, lemon peel, baking soda and salt; stir well. Stir in cranberries; spoon into prepared pan.

3. Bake 20 minutes or until light brown. Cool completely in pan on wire rack. Cut into 16 squares.

Makes 16 bars

Nutrients Per Serving (1 square)					
Calories	**104**	Cholesterol	**13mg**	Carbohydrate	**15g**
Sodium	**150mg**	Protein	**3g**	Fiber	**<1g**
Total fat	**3g**				

Lemon-Cranberry Bars

Currant Cheesecake Bars

½ **cup (1 stick) butter, softened**
 1 **cup all-purpose flour**
½ **cup packed light brown sugar**
½ **cup finely chopped pecans**
 1 **package (8 ounces) cream cheese, softened**
¼ **cup granulated sugar**
 1 **egg**
 1 **tablespoon milk**
 2 **teaspoons grated lemon peel**
⅓ **cup currant jelly or seedless raspberry jam**

Preheat oven to 350°F. Grease 9-inch square baking pan. Beat butter in medium bowl with electric mixer at medium speed until smooth. Add flour, brown sugar and pecans; beat at low speed until well blended. Press mixture into bottom and partially up sides of prepared pan.

Bake about 15 minutes or until light brown. If sides of crust have shrunk down, press back up and reshape with spoon. Let cool 5 minutes on wire rack.

Meanwhile, beat cream cheese in large bowl with electric mixer at medium speed until smooth. Add granulated sugar, egg, milk and lemon peel; beat until well blended.

Heat jelly in small saucepan over low heat 2 to 3 minutes or until smooth, stirring occasionally.

Pour cream cheese mixture over crust. Drizzle jelly in 7 to 8 horizontal strips across filling with spoon. Swirl jelly through filling with knife to create marbled effect.

Bake 20 to 25 minutes or until filling is set. Cool completely on wire rack before cutting into bars. Store in airtight container in refrigerator up to 1 week.   *Makes about 32 bars*

Nutrients Per Serving (1 bar)					
Calories	**105**	Cholesterol	**22mg**	Carbohydrate	**11g**
Sodium	**54mg**	Protein	**1g**	Fiber	**<1g**
Total fat	**7g**				

Currant Cheesecake Bars

Double Chocolate Brownies

1 cup EQUAL® SPOONFUL*
¾ cup all-purpose flour
½ cup semi-sweet chocolate chips or mini chocolate chips
6 tablespoons unsweetened cocoa powder
1 teaspoon baking powder
¼ teaspoon salt
6 tablespoons stick butter or margarine, softened
½ cup unsweetened applesauce
2 eggs
1 teaspoon vanilla

*May substitute 24 packets Equal® sweetener.

• Combine Equal®, flour, chocolate chips, cocoa, baking powder and salt. Beat butter, applesauce, eggs and vanilla until blended. Stir in flour mixture until blended.

• Spread batter in 8-inch square baking pan sprayed with nonstick cooking spray. Bake in preheated 350°F oven 18 to 20 minutes or until top springs back when gently touched. Cool completely on wire rack.

Makes 16 servings

Nutrients Per Serving (1 brownie)					
Calories	**108**	Cholesterol	**38mg**	Carbohydrate	**10g**
Sodium	**119mg**	Protein	**2g**	Fiber	**1g**
Total fat	**7g**				

Smart Tip

Unsweetened cocoa is formed by extracting most of the cocoa butter from pure chocolate and grinding the remaining chocolate solids into a powder. Since cocoa powder is naturally lower in fat than other chocolate baking ingredients, it is often used to make reduced-fat baked goods.

Double Chocolate Brownies

Luscious Lemon Bars

½ **cup plus 1 tablespoon graham cracker crumbs, divided**
¾ **cup SPLENDA® Granular, divided**
 2 **tablespoons light butter, melted**
 2 **tablespoons all-purpose flour**
½ **cup egg substitute**
½ **cup fat-free half-and-half**
½ **cup fresh lemon juice**
 1 **tablespoon fresh grated lemon peel**

1. Preheat oven to 350°F. Spray 8×8-inch baking pan with nonstick cooking spray. Set aside.

2. Mix ½ cup graham cracker crumbs, ¼ cup SPLENDA® and melted butter in small bowl. Stir until crumbs are well coated. Press firmly into prepared pan. Set aside.

3. Place remaining ½ cup SPLENDA® and flour in medium bowl; mix well. Add egg substitute and half-and-half; stir until blended. Slowly add lemon juice, stirring constantly. Stir in lemon peel.

4. Slowly pour mixture over graham cracker base. Bake in preheated oven 12 to 18 minutes or until set. Remove from oven and top with remaining 1 tablespoon graham cracker crumbs.

5. Chill in refrigerator 2 hours before serving.   *Makes 9 servings*

Nutrients Per Serving (1 bar)					
Calories	**70**	Cholesterol	**5mg**	Carbohydrate	**10g**
Sodium	**85mg**	Protein	**3g**	Fiber	**0g**
Total fat	**3g**				

Index

Acknowledgments

The publisher would like to thank the companies and organizations listed below for the use of their recipes and photographs in this publication.

Dole Food Company, Inc.

Equal® sweetener

Hershey Foods Corporation

Peanut Advisory Board

SPLENDA® is a trademark of McNeil PPC, Inc.